More FOR YOUR METHOD PIANO SERIES
A SUPPLEMENT TO ALL PIANO METHODS

Hal Leonard's "More For Your Method" series presents your favorite music in arrangements that use only those skills your method book teaches. The key on this page will even tell you at what point in your method you will be ready to play each piece!

After you find the method book you are using, choose the piece you wish to play. Use the key to discover what page in your method you have to complete before you will know everything you need to know to play that piece.

PRE-READING PIANO SOLOS IN FIVE-FINGER PATTERNS

First Christmas Carols

Arranged by Fred Kern

Edited by Barbara Kreader • Illustrated by Carol Horzempa

PAGE		Aaron Piano Primer	Alfred Prep Course Primer	Bastien Piano Lessons Primer	Bastien Piano/ Young Beginner Primer A/B	Bastien Piano Basics Primer	Clark Music Tree A	Gillock Piano All The Way	Glover-Stewart Method for Piano Primer	Noona Basic Piano Starter Book	Olson Pathways Book A	Pace Kinder-Keyboard	Schaum Piano Course Pre-A	Thompson Teaching Little Fingers
8	Away In The Manger	17	98	12	14 (B)	11	21	27 (1-A)	16	18	49	34	18	14
2	Good King Wenceslas	15	98	13	18 (A)	16	21	28 (1-A)	18	18	49	34	18	14
6	Jesus, Jesus, Rest Your Head	17	98	12	14 (B)	11	21	27 (1-A)	16	18	49	34	18	14
13	O Come All Ye Faithful	17	98	12	14 (B)	11	21	27 (1-A)	16	18	49	34	18	14
10	O Come, O Come, Emmanuel	36	98	48	19 (B)	35	34	24 (2)	26	40	39	24	31	24
4	We Three Kings of Orient Are	36	98	48	19 (B)	35	34	24 (2)	26	40	39	24	31	24

HAL•LEONARD® CORPORATION
7777 W. BLUEMOUND RD. P.O. BOX 13819 MILWAUKEE, WI 53213

T0051143

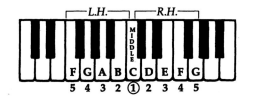

Good King Wenceslas

Traditional

Like a march

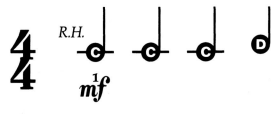
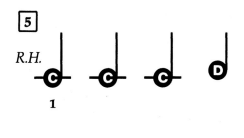
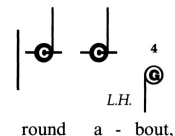
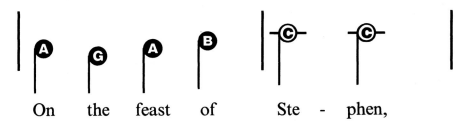
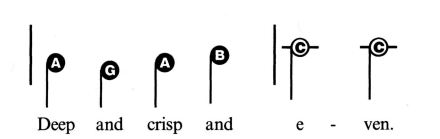

Good King Wen - ces - las looked out, On the feast of Ste - phen,

When the snow lay round a - bout, Deep and crisp and e - ven.

Duet Part (Student plays one octave higher)

Like a march

staccato

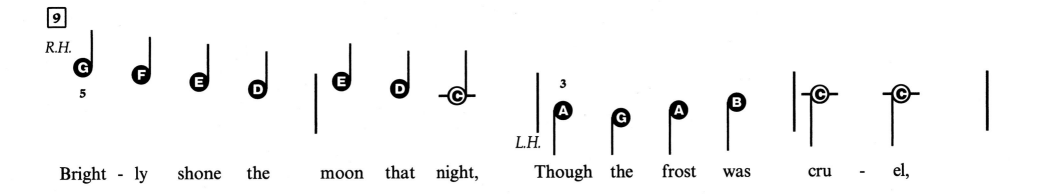

9

R.H.

Bright - ly   shone   the   moon   that   night,   Though   the   frost   was   cru - el,

13

When   a   poor   man   came   in   sight,   Gath-'ring   win - ter   fu - el.

9

legato

13

staccato

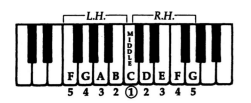

We Three Kings of Orient Are

John Henry Hopkins

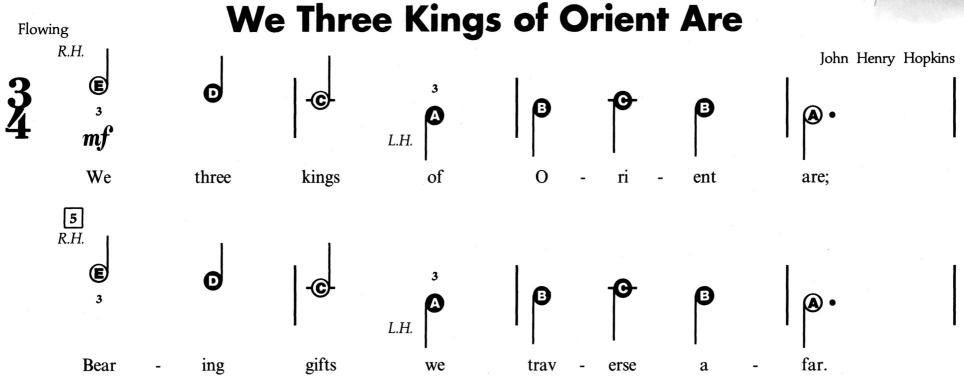

We three kings of O - ri - ent are;

Bear - ing gifts we trav - erse a - far.

Duet Part (Student plays one octave higher)

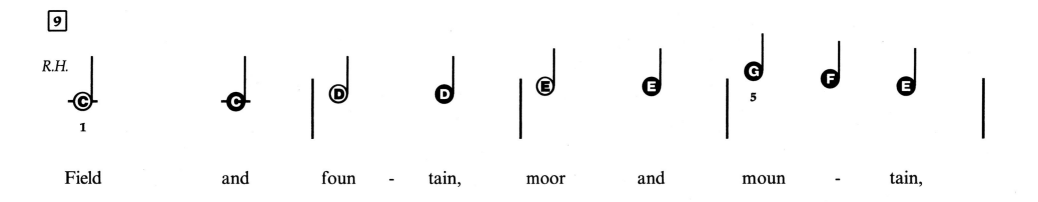

Field and foun - tain, moor and moun - tain,

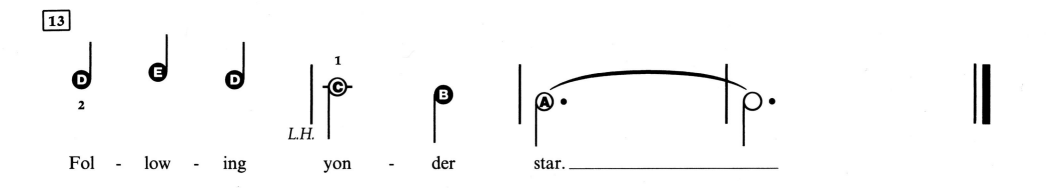

Fol - low - ing yon - der star.

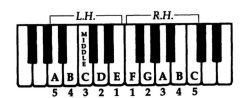

Jesus, Jesus, Rest Your Head

Quietly

Appalachian

Je - sus, Je - sus, rest your head. You have got a man - ger bed.

Duet Part (Student plays one octave higher)

Quietly

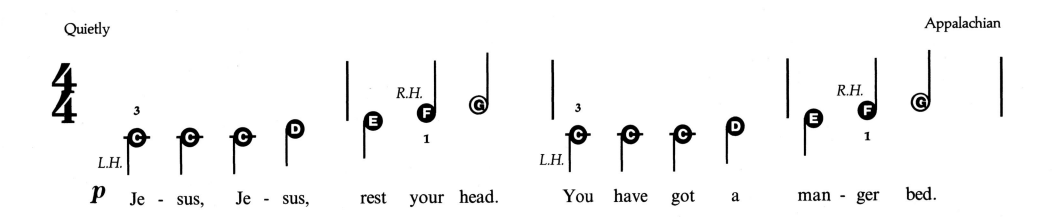

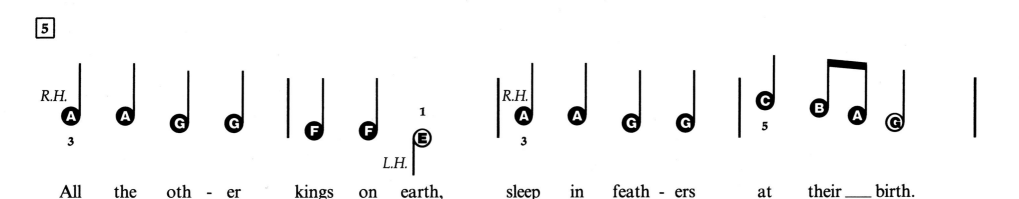

All the oth - er kings on earth, sleep in feath - ers at their ___ birth.

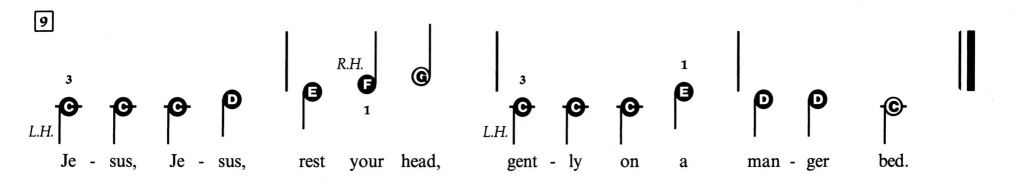

Je - sus, Je - sus, rest your head, gent - ly on a man - ger bed.

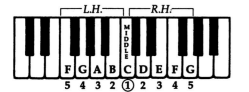

Away in a Manger

James Murray

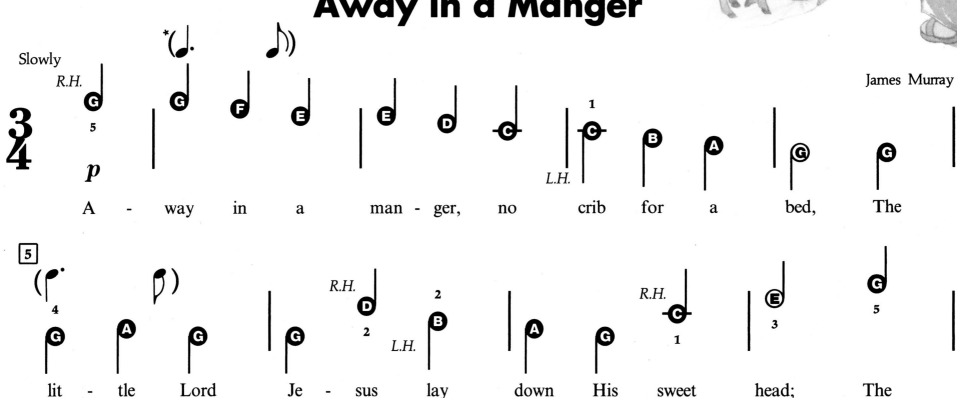

A - way in a man - ger, no crib for a bed, The

lit - tle Lord Je - sus lay down His sweet head; The

*Teachers' Note: Once students have read the rhythm as written, they may wish to add patterns in parentheses by rote.

Duet Part (Student plays one octave higher)

Slowly

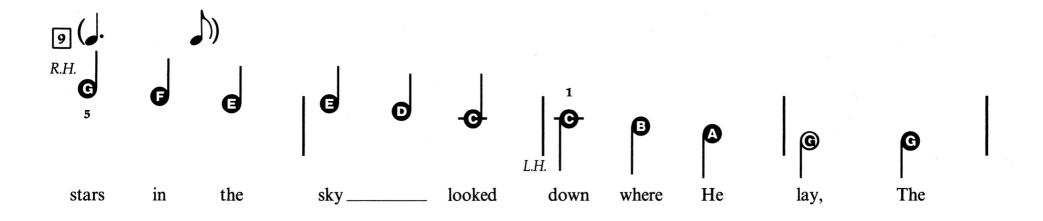

stars   in   the   sky_____   looked   down   where   He   lay,   The

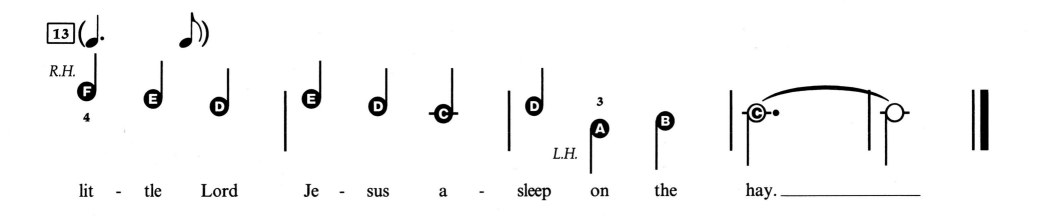

lit - tle   Lord   Je - sus   a - sleep   on   the   hay._____

O Come, O Come Emmanuel

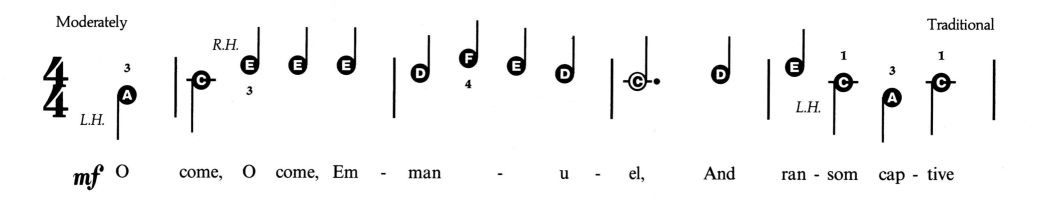

Moderately

Traditional

mf O come, O come, Em - man - u - el, And ran - som cap - tive

Duet Part (Student plays one octave higher)

Moderately

With pedal

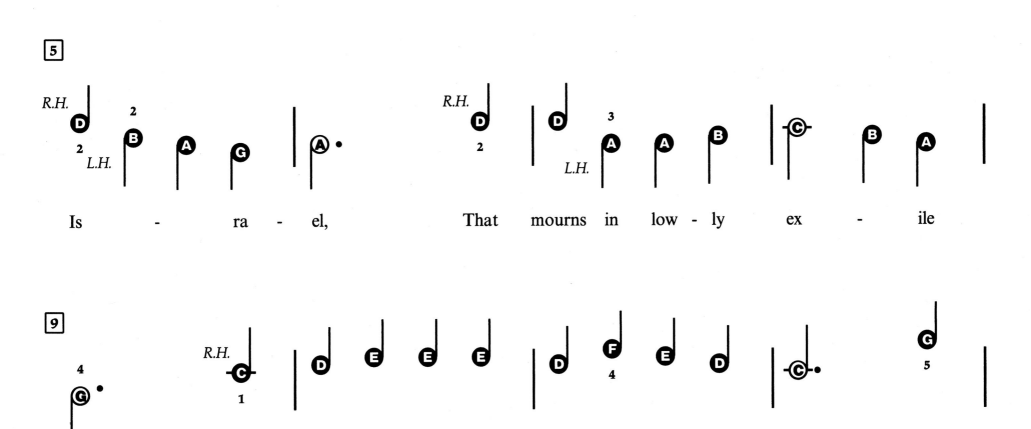

5   Is -   ra -   el,   That   mourns   in   low - ly   ex -   ile

9   here,   Un - til   the   Son   of   God _____ ap - pear.   Re -

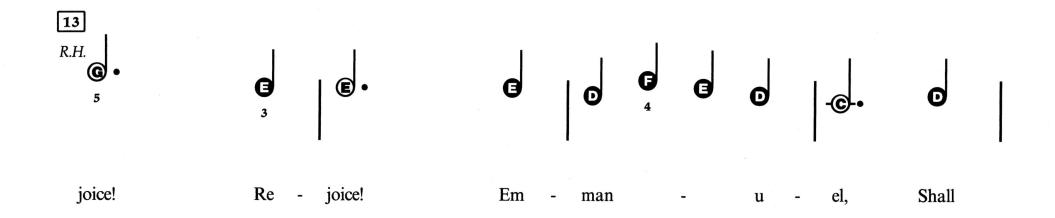

joice!   Re - joice!   Em - man - u - el,   Shall

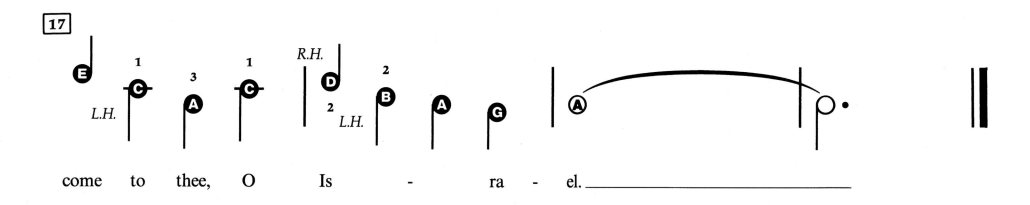

come to thee, O Is - ra - el. _____

O Come, All Ye Faithful

J.F. Wade

O come, all ye faith - ful, joy - ful and tri - um - phant, O

*Teachers' Note: Once students have read the rhythm as written, they may wish to add patterns in parentheses by rote.

Duet Part (Student plays one octave higher)

Moderately

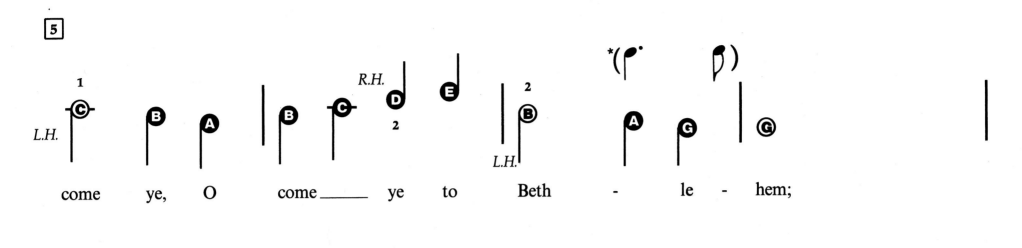

come ye, O come   ye to Beth - le - hem;

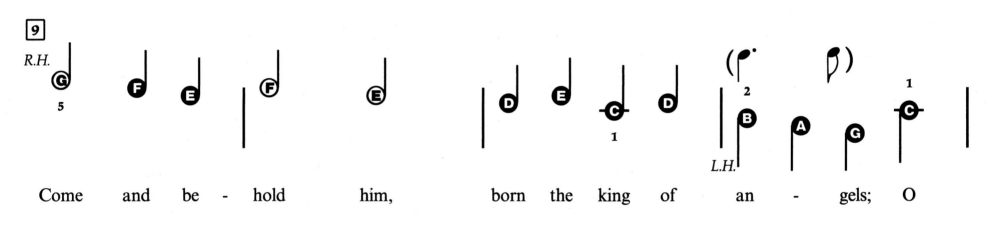

Come and be - hold him, born the king of an - gels; O

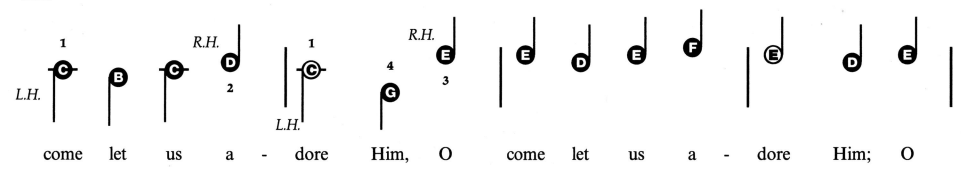

come   let   us   a - dore   Him,   O   come   let   us   a - dore   Him;   O

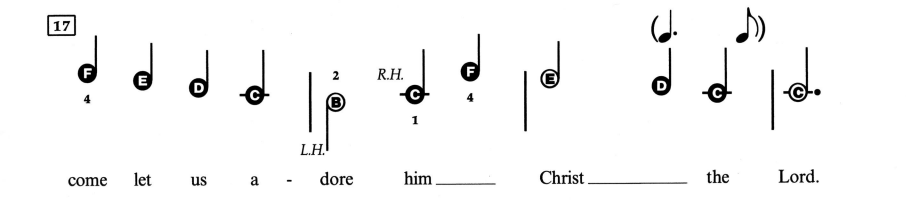

come   let   us   a - dore   him _____   Christ _____   the   Lord.